Runaway Jew - The Truth about Jonah

This book largely draws (unless otherwise indicated) upon the NASB Scripture quotations taken from the New American Standard Bible®, Copyright © 1960, 1962, 1963, 1968, 1971, 1972, 1973, 1975, 1977, 1995 by The Lockman Foundation. Used by permission.

Templehouse Publishing ISBN 9781913495077

Copyright © 2021-05-01 Dr A .T. Bradford

Published by Templehouse Publishing, London, England.

For other titles by this author please visit our website:

www.templehouse-publishing.com

Introduction

'Those who sail the sea tell stories of its dangers, which astonish all who hear them; in it are strange and wonderful creatures, all kinds of living things and huge sea-monsters. By his own action he [God] achieves his ends.' (Ecclesiasticus 43:25-26).

Almost everyone knows the story of Jonah and the 'whale'.

The greatest Jew ever to walk on earth (Jesus of Nazareth) figuratively offered Jonah as a 'sign' to the ruling Temple authorities, in relation to his own ministry.

But who was Jonah? And was there really a whale? Why is Jonah so important? And what does he have to do with Jesus?

Historic Background

Jonah hails from c 900 BC. Like Jesus of Nazareth, he was a Galilean, from Gath-hepher in Northern Israel (2 Kings 14:25). Jonah's story is recounted annually every Yom-Kippur, as part of religious Jews' annual self-evaluation of their personal life choices and social contributions.

900-600BC was also the time of the mighty Assyrian Empire. Assyria was a kind of USSR of the Middle-Eastern ancient world, with the region's most powerful army, one strengthened by their recent advances in iron weaponry and chariots. Like the Romans later would, they deployed military engineers, mobile siege ladders and ramps. Like the much later Ottomans and Europeans, they utilised sappers and miners to undermine enemy city walls.

A warrior people with compulsory military service for all their young men, they conquered and ruled an empire stretching (east-west) from North Africa to Iran, and (south-north) from the Arabian Peninsula to Armenia.

By the twelfth century BC they had conquered Babylon, demolishing its walls and raiding its temple. By the time of the prophet Jonah they had developed a fearsome reputation for ruthlessness and cruelty, conducting many genocides, massacres, wholesale ethnic cleansings, mass deportations and mutilations (including skinning their enemies alive). By 705 BC, Nineveh was their capital.

And it was to wicked Nineveh that God commanded his prophet Jonah to go and preach repentance.

Is it any wonder that Jonah was reluctant to obey?

Jonah 1

1:1-3 'The word of the Lord came to Jonah the son of Amittai saying, "Arise, go to Nineveh the great city and cry against it, for their wickedness has come up before me." But Jonah rose up to flee to Tarshish from the presence of the Lord. So he went down to Joppa, found a ship which was going to Tarshish, paid the fare and went down into it to go with them to Tarshish from the presence of the Lord.'

'Lord' in Hebrew is *'Yahweh'*, by whose unspeakable tetragramic name the universe was created.

Jonah's father's name Ammitai is the Hebrew word for 'true', from *'emet'*, meaning 'faithful'. Jonah's own name, by contrast, is the Hebrew word for 'dove' or 'pigeon'.

God's command that Jonah 'cry' (Hebrew: *'qara'* - 'read'/'proclaim') against the Assyrian city of Nineveh (in modern day Iraq) is rather like asking a Jew in 1930's Germany to preach against Hitler and National Socialism. Unsurprisingly, given the Assyrians' savage history, Jonah does what has served Jews well down their centuries of oppression and persecution - he flees.

Tarshish in southern Iberia (the Jewish-Roman historian has 'Tarsus' in Turkey) was in the exact opposite direction to Nineveh, and about as far as it was possible to go.

Since God is omnipresent, Jonah would most have certainly known it was impossible to escape from his presence. Perhaps he simply wanted to delay what he later claimed to have foreseen, the application of divine mercy to an indisputably sinful people. Less possibly, he was simply being wilful, defiant and disobedient.

1:4-6 'The Lord hurled a great wind on the sea and there was a great storm on the sea so that the ship was about to break up. Then the sailors became afraid and every man cried to his god, and they threw the cargo which was in the ship into the sea to lighten it for them. But Jonah had gone below into the hold of the ship, lain down and fallen sound asleep. So the captain approached him and said, "How is it that you are sleeping? Get up, call on your god. Perhaps your god will be concerned about us so that we will not perish."

The Mediterranean Sea off Israel's coast is renowned for its violent gusts of wind. Ultimately, these are all under God's control, but this one was especially so, a small reminder to Jonah of who exactly it was that he was messing with.

Psalm 104:5 describes the sea as being the world's 'garment' or 'robe.'

The sleeping Jonah was about to become entangled in one of God's robes!

The accompanying storm, of the type that had helped shape the Jews' wholesale distrust of oceans, was also doing its (un)level best to destroy them all. While the crew panic, the recalcitrant prophet, exhausted, depressed, or both, is napping. It is the ship's captain who is spiritually concerned for others' welfare, one of the narrative's many little ironies.

1:7-9 'Each man said to his mate, "Come, let us cast lots so we may learn on whose account this calamity has struck us. "So they cast lots and the lot fell on Jonah. Then they said to him, "Tell us, now! On whose account has this calamity struck us? What is your occupation? And where do you come from? What is your country? From what, people are you?" He said to them, "I am a Hebrew, and I fear the Lord God of heaven who made the sea and the dry land."''

'Casting the lot' is a Hebrew traditional form of sortition, a method of establishing divine guidance using apparently random means, such as rolling dice or drawing out straws of differing length.

God himself had instituted it (Leviticus 16:8), and Moses had employed it in allocating land to the tribes of Israel (Numbers 26:55) as, much later, had Jesus' disciples (Acts 1:26).

The crew having thereby identified Jonah as the underlying problem, Jonah underscores and validates their findings still further by emphasising God's very particular interest in, and involvement with, the sea itself.

1:10-14 'Then the men became extremely, frightened and they said to him, "How could you do this?" For the men knew that he was fleeing from the presence of the Lord, because he had told them. So they said to him, "What should we do to you that the sea may become calm for us?" - for the sea was becoming increasingly stormy. He said to them, "Pick me up and throw me into the sea. Then the sea will become calm for you, for I know that on account of me this great storm has come upon you." However, the men rowed desperately to return to land but they could not, for the sea was becoming even stormier against them. Then they called on the Lord and said, "We earnestly pray, O Lord, do not let us perish on account of this man's life and do not put innocent blood on us; for you, O Lord, have done as you have pleased."'

Once again, the pagan crew members prove themselves to be more caring and spiritually minded than Israel's prophet. Jonah however, now demonstrates what is either severe depression with suicidal ideation or supreme trust in the Almighty.

Jonah is missing from the roll call of Jewish faith-greats found in Hebrews chapter 11, but this author believes that his knowledge of and trust in Yahweh, in the self-evident willingness to lay down his life, perhaps warrants his inclusion therein.

'Pick me up and throw me in the sea' may be seen as a faith statement almost on a par with Jesus' blood-soaked prayer in the Garden of Gethsemane - 'Not my will but yours be done' (Mark 14:36 and Luke 22:42). While their motives were undoubtedly very different, both Jonah and Jesus were willing to give up their lives, trusting that God's overriding purpose would be thereby fulfilled.

Unaware of the spiritual significance, the pagan crew redouble their futile efforts to escape the storm, using oars before capitulating to what even they recognise as being God's will. Their prayer reveals their own underlying purity of spirit, again, notable for pagan non-Jews.

1:15-16 'So they picked up Jonah, threw him into the sea, and the sea stopped its raging. Then the men feared the Lord greatly, and they offered a sacrifice to the Lord and made vows.'

The God who would later calm and even walk in bodily form as Messiah upon the turbulent waters of Lake Galilee instantly withdrew the power of the storm.

Just as Jesus' disciples later did, the crew 'feared' God in reverence and awe, expressed in an offering. The Hebrew word here for 'vows' is *'neder'*, meaning 'votive offerings'. These were items that were considered sacred and placed as reminders of a divine intervention.

1:17 'And the Lord appointed a great fish to swallow Jonah, and Jonah was in the stomach of the fish three days and three nights.'

Legend holds that it was a 'whale' that swallowed the (now dead) body of the prophet. Whatever variety of marine life it was is less relevant than its ability to accommodate Jonah's lifeless form in its belly.

'Days' is, in Hebrew, *'yom'*, and 'nights' is *'layil'*. Both constitute an *'omer'* - a common Talmudic legal unit of 'measurement or portion'. This, when applied to time, may range from a few moments to many hours. A few minutes followed by an entire 24 hour period, followed by a few more minutes legally constitute three *'omer'* - three 'days and nights'.

This has a special significance with regard to Jesus' death and resurrection:

Luke 11:29-32 'And while the crowds were thickly gathered together, he began to say, "This is an evil generation. It seeks a sign, and no sign will be given to it except the sign of Jonah the prophet. For as Jonah became a sign to the Ninevites, so also the Son of Man will be to this generation. The Queen of the South will rise up in the judgment with the men of this generation and condemn them, for she came from the ends of the earth to hear the wisdom of Solomon; and indeed a greater than Solomon is here. The men of Nineveh will rise up in the judgment with this generation and condemn it, for they repented at the preaching of Jonah; and indeed a greater than Jonah is here."'

The parallel passage in Matthew's earlier Gospel (chapter 12) clarifies this prophetic sign as being specifically related to the three 'days and nights' that both Jonah and Jesus spent in Sheol, the Hebrew's place of the dead.

Jonah 2

2:1-2 'Then Jonah prayed to the Lord his God from the fish's belly. And he said:'

The narrative details that follow show conclusively that Jonah was, by this point, physically dead. Human beings are made in God's image and have a spirit-life that, like God's, is eternal in nature.

It cannot die and must therefore exist forever.

The only question is where.

This (Hebrew) view is reflected in the account of King Saul's encounter with the dead prophet Samuel (1 Samuel 28) and also in Jesus' parable of the rich man and Lazarus (Luke 16), where the dead rich man (traditionally known as 'Dives') expresses spiritual concern for his still-living siblings.

In this passage, the still-living spirit of the now (physically) dead Jonah is communicating with God from the belly of the fish.

22 'I cried out to the Lord because of my affliction,
And he answered me.
"Out of the belly of Sheol I cried,
And you heard my voice.'

Sheol is the Hebrew for the place of the dead. Jonah had sunk to the Mediterranean seabed (verse 6), where seaweed grew (verse 5). At such depths, the 'great fish' had simply hoovered his limp body up. But Jonah's spirit was still able to pray. King David's earlier prayers, including Psalm 18, appear to have clearly shaped Jonah's.

Psalms 18:4-7 'The cords of death encompassed me,
And the torrents of ungodliness terrified me. The cords of Sheol surrounded me;
The snares of death confronted me. In my distress I called upon the Lord,
And cried to my God for help;
He heard my voice out of his temple,
And my cry for help before him came into his ears.
Then the earth shook and quaked;
And the foundations of the mountains were trembling.'

The God who makes 'the darkness of waters his hiding place' (Psalm 18:11) was waiting to meet Jonah at the bottom of the sea.

From inside the stomach of the fish, the now-dead Jonah's prayer-time continued:

3: 'For you cast me into the deep, into the heart of the seas. And the floods surrounded me; all your breakers and your billows passed over me.'

The sons of Korah's Psalm (Psalm 42) now features in Jonah's prayer:

Psalms 42:7-8 'Deep calls to deep at the sound of your waterfalls; all your breakers and your billows have rolled over me. The Lord will command his loving-kindness in the daytime; and his song will be with me in the night, a prayer to the God of my life.'

This prayer, penned approximately 200 years earlier, perfectly summed up Jonah's predicament. Covered by God's waves, he experienced God commanding his (covenant-based) love…

In the form of a 'great fish.' (Hebrew: *'gadowl dag'*, whales not inhabiting the region!).

2: 4: 'Then I said, 'I have been cast out of your sight;
Yet I will look again toward your holy temple.'

The magnificent Temple of Solomon had not long been completed, and Jonah was confident, in death, that he will see it again (in life). Though out of sight, he was clearly very much still in God's mind.

2: 5: 'The waters surrounded me, even to my soul;
The deep closed around me;
Weeds were wrapped around my head.'

'Weeds' is the Hebrew word *'suph'*, also meaning 'rushes'. Jonah encountered these root-bearing plants on the Mediterranean seabed to which he had sunk after being forcibly ejected from the ship.

'Soul' is *'nephesh'*, the Hebrew word for the life-essence of mankind themselves. Jonah is describing the point of his entry into Sheol, the underworld occupied by the spirits of the dead.

2: 6: 'I went down to the roots of the mountains;
The earth with its bars closed behind me forever;
Yet you have brought up my life from the pit,
O Lord, my God.'

Mountains and indeed all dry land arise ultimately from the seabed, which, in the case of the Mediterranean, is more than 5000 metres below the surface. Water pressure at such depths utterly crushes a human corpse. Fortunately for Jonah, the God who 'redeems life from the pit' (Job 33:18 and Psalm 103:4) was not constrained by such natural obstacles.

2: 7: 'When my soul fainted within me,
I remembered the Lord;
And my prayer went up to you,
Into your holy temple.'

'Fainted' is *'ataph'* - to be 'overcome by weakness'. Dying did not prevent Jonah's soul and spirit from reaching out to his Creator. His prayers were received and heard in God's throne room.

2: 8: 'Those who regard worthless idols
Forsake their own mercy.'

A common view about the afterlife is that one's good deeds somehow facilitate one's entrance and acceptance there. While this is certainly true of deeds done in faith, 'worthless idolatry' (literally, 'deceptive and empty vanities') can render even human good deeds of very little value. As with all human endeavours towards pleasing God out of one's own strength, God is not impressed. One's own 'mercy' ('*chesed*'- 'acts of kindness') being of no eternal value. As the Jewish prophet Isaiah would later pray, to God, 'all our good deeds are as filthy rags.' (Isaiah 64:6).

2: 9: 'But I will sacrifice to you
With the voice of thanksgiving;
I will pay what I have vowed.
Salvation is of the Lord.'

Experiencing death clearly sharpened the prophet's spiritual focus, such that he is already in faith for and anticipating offering sacrifices and praise in the Temple of Solomon in Jerusalem.

He is now also determined to make good on earlier apparent promises of obedience, even though underlying character flaws would, sadly, persist...

There is more than a whiff of God's sense of humour in the final line. 'Salvation' is, in the Hebrew, '*yeshuah*', the name announced to the tekton Joseph by the Angel Gabriel to be given to the Messiah himself (Matthew 1:21).

The last line of verse 9 therefore actually reads, 'Jesus is from Yahweh'.

2:10 'Then the Lord commanded the fish, and it vomited Jonah up onto the dry land.'

Fish appear to have less problem obeying God than do some prophets. When God raised Jonah back to life, his consequential bodily movement triggered a nerve-based reflex in the fish - vomiting.

Jonah 3

3:1-4 'Now the word of the Lord came to Jonah the second time, saying, "Arise, go to Nineveh the great city and proclaim to it the proclamation which I am going to tell you." So Jonah arose and went to Nineveh according to the word of the Lord. Now Nineveh was an exceedingly great city, a three days' walk. Then Jonah began to go through the city one day's walk; and he cried out and said, "Yet forty days and Nineveh will be overthrown."

Chapter 2 does not record the location of the 'dry land' where the fish regurgitated its unusual meal; however the event was almost certainly witnessed. Eye-witness accounts would therefore have supported Jonah's (very brief and perhaps rather incomplete) message's reception in the Assyrian capital.

3:5-9 'Then the people of Nineveh believed in God; and they called a fast and put on sackcloth from the greatest to the least of them. When the word reached the King of Nineveh, he arose from his throne, laid aside his robe from him, covered himself with sackcloth and sat on the ashes. He issued a proclamation and it said, "In Nineveh by the decree of the king and his nobles: Do not let man, beast, herd, or flock taste a thing. Do not let them eat or drink water. But both man and beast must be covered with sackcloth; and let men call on God earnestly that each may turn from his wicked way and from the violence which is in his hands. Who knows, God may turn and relent and withdraw his burning anger so that we will not perish."

Fasting, with sackcloth, dust and ashes, were outward signs of mourning, in this case for sin. Even the king descended from his throne to participate, along with all the animals. The Hebrew for 'perish' (*'abad'*), may also be translated as 'annihilation' or 'destruction', something that the Assyrians had much experience of inflicting upon others. 'Violence' was second nature to them, and they were understandably keen to avoid God's fierce and intense wrath.

3:10 'When God saw their deeds, that they turned from their wicked way, then God relented concerning the calamity which he had declared he would bring upon them. And he did not do it.'

When man repents; God often relents, sometimes mistranslated as 'repents'. The Hebrew is *'nacham'*, meaning 'to change one's mind and console', instead of punishing.

God is gracious and merciful by nature. He does not wish to endlessly chastise. His grace, however, is not without end.

One day in the mid seventh century AD, the Assyrian empire came to an end, to be replaced by the recently inspired invading Arab Islamists.

God's ultimate expression of grace would eventually fully come later, c 5BC, in human form, in the person of the long-awaited Messiah, Jesus of Nazareth.

Jonah 4

1-4 'But it greatly displeased Jonah and he became angry. He prayed to the Lord and said, "Please Lord, was not this what I said while I was still in my own country? Therefore, in order to forestall this I fled to Tarshish, for I knew that you are a gracious and compassionate God, slow to anger and abundant in loving-kindness, and one who relents concerning calamity. Therefore now, O Lord, please take my life from me, for death is better to me than life." The Lord said, "Do you have good reason to be angry?"'

Finally, the Hebrew text provides Jonah's side of the story. The prophet knew very well the merciful and forgiving nature of the God he served.

God's revelation of himself to Moses had emphasised the essential nature of his being - compassion, grace and pity/mercy.

Exodus 34:6 'Then the Lord passed by in front of him and proclaimed, "The Lord, the Lord God, compassionate and gracious, slow to anger, and abounding in loving-kindness and truth."'

'Compassion' in Hebrew is *'raham'*, meaning 'to show mercy/pity'. This quality is at the heart of who God is, and King David had earlier likened it to the emotion that a father feels towards his own children - a loving care mixed with pity and concern for their weak state, that moves the father to help them in their need. This is especially pertinent given God's later reference to children (in verse 11).

Psalm 103: 8-13:

'The Lord is compassionate and gracious,
slow to anger and abounding in loving-kindness.
He will not always strive with us,
nor will He keep his anger forever.
He has not dealt with us according to our sins, nor rewarded us according to our iniquities.
For as high as the heavens are above the earth,
so great is his loving-kindness toward those who fear him.
As far as the east is from the west,
so far has he removed our transgressions from us.
Just as a father has compassion on his children,
so the Lord has compassion on those who fear him.'

Jonah understood all of this extremely well, and had actually anticipated that his merciful God would let the Ninevites off the consequences of their horrendous actions. And Jonah's (righteous) anger against the Ninevites was such that he didn't want that to happen.

Consequently he had deliberately travelled in the opposite direction. Even after experiencing death and the grace of bodily resurrection, he remained stuck in this (righteous) anger.

In his own mind, he did indeed have reason to be angry.

But was it a 'good' reason?

Much later Jesus would challenge a fellow religious Jew over his use of the word 'good'. 'Why do you call me good? Who is good but God alone?' (Mark 10:18).

Only God has the right and the ability to define what constitutes goodness. For Jonah, hundreds of years prior to Messiah's arrival, the concept of unearned favour (grace) had yet to be fully expressed.

To Jonah, the Assyrians were deeply evil and beyond redemption. To God, **both** Jews and Assyrians were sinful human beings. The differences that seemed so enormous to Jonah barely registered in comparison with the majesty of God's own eternal nature and supreme being.

By this point in the narrative Jonah is tired and fed up, conflicted between what he knows; God's merciful nature on the one hand, and the need for justice and the righting of wrongs on the other. Instead of arguing with the Almighty, Jonah prefers to give up.

But, rather than be unduly hasty, the prophet decides to wait a while.

5-6 'Then Jonah went out from the city and sat east of it. There he made a shelter for himself and sat under it in the shade until, he could see what would happen in the city. So the Lord God appointed a plant and it grew up over, Jonah to be a shade over his head to deliver him from his discomfort. And Jonah was extremely happy about the plant.'

Previously Israel's very tired prophet Elijah had been cared for by angels (1 Kings 19). Even God-appointed (though ritually unclean) ravens had earlier helped out (1 Kings 17)!

Jonah was evidently a man of self-reliance and independent action. He built his own shelter, which quickly became unbearably hot under the blazing Iraqi sun.

God in his kindness 'appointed' a shade-providing plant to grow over Jonah's shelter. This alleviated the prophet's discomfort, for which Jonah was deeply appreciative.

The Hebrew for 'appointed' is *'manah'*, meaning to 'prepare and number off'. God had firstly prepared a prophet, but the prophet had exercised his God-given freewill by running away. God then prepared a storm, a fish and a plant, all of which obeyed him. He would soon prepare an equally obedient worm and a scorching wind.

All of this because Jonah was extremely valuable to God, both as his child and as his prophet. Jonah was far too valuable to be allowed to wallow in self-pity and in his somewhat incomplete notions concerning spiritual concepts such as grace and mercy.

7-8 'But God appointed a worm when dawn came the next day and it attacked the plant and it withered. When the sun came up God appointed a scorching east wind, and the sun beat down on Jonah's head so that he became faint and begged with all his soul to die, saying, "Death is better to me than life."'

Desert winds in Iraq are notoriously hot. After the appointed worm had caused the appointed plant to die, Jonah was left experiencing the full force of the extreme heat, such that he became emotionally and physically overcome and even downright suicidal. Severe depression coupled with physical weakness is a well recognised cause of loss of hope, and the prophet appears to have come, finally, to the end of his tether. And finally, in that moment, come to a place of greater understanding of God himself.

9-11 'Then God said to Jonah, "Do you have good reason to be angry about the plant?" And he said, "I have good reason to be angry, even to death." Then the Lord said, "You had compassion on the plant for which you did not work and which you did not cause to grow, which came up overnight, and perished overnight. Should I not have compassion on Nineveh, the great city in which there are more than 120,000, persons who do not know the difference between their right and left hand, as well as many animals?"'

Jonah's anger had gradually and subtly switched from being righteous to being unrighteous. Gone was his godly indignation towards the pagan Assyrians over their many terrible atrocities towards others, now replaced by an all too human unrighteous anger born out of his own tiredness, self-pity and frustration.

These he experienced both towards the loss of the plant and also the loss of his much-anticipated satisfaction at seeing a dramatic Sodom and Gomorrah type of judgement upon Nineveh.

People who 'didn't know the difference between their right and left hand' were infants, and/or those mentally infirm. God's compassion and concern is greater towards them than to the rest of the general population. It even included divine compassion and mercy towards animals, themselves innocent of the Assyrians' sins.

Afternote

Psalm 107 could have been written partly with Jonah in mind:

Psalm 107:1-9:
'Oh, give thanks to the Lord, for he is good!
For His mercy endures forever.
Let the redeemed of the Lord say so,
Whom He has redeemed from the hand of the enemy,
And gathered out of the lands,
From the east and from the west,
From the north and from the south.
They wandered in the wilderness in a desolate way;
They found no city to dwell in.
Hungry and thirsty,
Their soul fainted in them.
Then they cried out to the Lord in their trouble,
And he delivered them out of their distresses.
And he led them forth by the right way,
That they might go to a city for a dwelling place.
Oh, that men would give thanks to the Lord for his goodness,
And for his wonderful works to the children of men!
For he satisfies the longing soul,
And fills the hungry soul with goodness.'

10: *'Those who sat in darkness and in the shadow of death,*

Bound in affliction and irons.'

11-14a: 'Because they rebelled against the words of God,
And despised the counsel of the Most High,
Therefore he brought down their heart with labour;
They fell down, and there was none to help.
Then they cried out to the Lord in their trouble,
And he saved them out of their distresses.
He brought them out of darkness and the shadow of death,'

And broke their chains in pieces.
Oh, that men would give thanks to the Lord for his goodness,
And for his wonderful works to the children of men!
For he has broken the gates of bronze,
And cut the bars of iron in two.
Fools, because of their transgression,
And because of their iniquities, were afflicted.
Their soul abhorred all manner of food,
And they drew near to the gates of death.
Then they cried out to the Lord in their trouble,
And he saved them out of their distresses.
He sent His word and healed them,
And delivered them from their destructions.
Oh, that men would give thanks to the Lord for his goodness,
And for his wonderful works to the children of men!

Let them sacrifice the sacrifices of thanksgiving,
And declare his works with rejoicing.

23-29: 'Those who go down to the sea in ships,
Who do business on great waters,
 They see the works of the Lord,
And his wonders in the deep.
For he commands and raises the stormy wind,
Which lifts up the waves of the sea.
They mount up to the heavens,
They go down again to the depths;
Their soul melts because of trouble.
They reel to and fro, and stagger like a drunken man,
And are at their wits' end.
Then they cry out to the Lord in their trouble,
And he brings them out of their distresses.
He calms the storm,
So that its waves are still'.

God had calmed the storm by the rather drastic measure of having Jonah thrown into it.

30-43: 'Then they are glad because they are quiet;
So He guides them to their desired haven.
 Oh, that men would give thanks to the Lord for his goodness,
And his wonderful works to the children of men!
Let them exalt him also in the assembly of the people,
And praise him in the company of the elders.

He turns rivers into a wilderness,
And the water-springs into dry ground;
A fruitful land into barrenness,
For the wickedness of those who dwell in it.
He turns a wilderness into pools of water,
And dry land into water-springs.
There he makes the hungry dwell,
That they may establish a city for a dwelling place,
And sow fields and plant vineyards,
That they may yield a fruitful harvest.
He also blesses them, and they multiply greatly;
And he does not let their cattle decrease.
When they are diminished and brought low
Through oppression, affliction and sorrow,
He pours contempt on princes,
And causes them to wander in the wilderness where there is no way;
Yet he sets the poor on high, far from affliction,
And makes their families like a flock.
The righteous see it and rejoice,
And all iniquity stops its mouth.
*Whoever is wise will observe these things,
And they will understand the loving-kindness of the Lord.'*

God took Jonah to Nineveh by a very unusual route, so that his reluctant prophet might better 'understand the loving-kindness of the Lord.'

Jonah is a 4-chapter book, but a type of chapter 5 exists within the teachings of Jesus of Nazareth.

Jesus taught extensively about the reality of God's judgment of all who reject his grace and offer of personal salvation.

In Jesus' day there was a prominent class of religious scholar known as the Pharisees, who oversaw the civil application of Jewish religious law in conjunction with their (textual scholar) Scribes.

These were men extremely well versed in the Jews' Oral Law, the product of centuries of rabbinic teaching dating from Moses' time. They regarded themselves as God's custodians of the law, holding 'the keys of God's kingdom' (Matthew 23:13) and determining exactly who had access to it (themselves), and by what means (the Oral Torah Law, as defined by them).

Their arrogance and self-righteousness drew some of Jesus' strongest condemnations. In doing so, Jesus compared these ultra-religious Jews unfavourably with the inhabitants of Nineveh.

As Jesus' disciple Matthew (himself a former Scribe) recorded:

'Then some of the Scribes and Pharisees answered, saying, "Teacher, we want to see a sign from you" But he answered and said to them, "An evil and adulterous generation seeks after a sign, and no sign will be given to it except the sign of the prophet Jonah. For as Jonah was three days and three nights in the belly of the great fish, so will the Son of Man be three days and three nights in the heart of the earth. The men of Nineveh will rise up in the judgment with this generation and condemn it, because they repented at the preaching of Jonah; and indeed a greater than Jonah is here. The queen of the South will rise up in the judgment with this generation and condemn it, for she came from the ends of the earth to hear the Wisdom of Solomon; and indeed a greater than Solomon is here."' (Matthew 12:38-42).

The tragic rejection of Jesus by his fellow religious Jews would lead to the cataclysmic Roman invasion of 65AD and the destruction of Herod's Temple in 70AD, followed by Israel's dispersion among the nations.

In Jonah's case, the pagan sailors and the Ninevites proved themselves to be more righteous than the Hebrew prophet himself.

The book of Jonah closes with God asking Jonah a question about priorities, including God's divine right to show mercy.

When God speaks to us, how do we respond?

Further titles by Dr Bradford from Templehouse Publishing:

'The New Testament On Women - What Every Man Should Know. ISBN 9780956479815

'The Jesus Discovery – Another Look At Christ's Missing Years' - Joseph the Temple 'Tekton' and Jesus the 'Didaskalos'. ISBN 9780956479808

'Ell Descubrimiento de Jesus, Otra Mirada a los Anos Perdidos de Cristo.' (The Spanish edition of 'The Jesus Discovery'). ISBN 9780956479846

'According To Matthew' - A Commentary on the Gospel Of Matthew. ISBN 9780956479839

'The Letter to The Hebrews' - A Commentary On The Book Of Hebrews. ISBN 9780956479853

'Adam, Saint or Sinner' - Adam as a 'type' of Christ (Romans 5:14). ISBN 9780956479860

'The Medical Gospel Of Luke, As Told To Him By Mary The Mother Of Jesus' ISBN 9780956479877

'Joseph in John, Judas and Jewish Jokes', a Commentary on John's Gospel. ISBN 978132655647981

'Second best Jew?' - a Commentary on the Apostle Paul and the Book of Acts. ISBN 9781913495053

All these titles are available with a money-back guarantee when purchased directly from the publisher via Templehouse-publishing.com.

They are available in print and digital format.

Other video and audio media formats are available free of charge on YouTube (search for 'Jesus tekton').

www.ingramcontent.com/pod-product-compliance
Lightning Source LLC
Chambersburg PA
CBHW060347250426
43669CB00056B/2548